T H E
FACTS

Scottish *Referendum*

Edited By Julie Simpson & Walter Donald

C

The Facts: Scottish Referendum
978-1908885470
Edited by Julie Simpson & Walter Donald

Published by Cargo Publishing 2014
SC376700

Printed & Bound in Scotland by Bell & Bain
Cover design and typeset by Cargo Publishing

www.cargopublishing.com

Also available as:
Kindle Ebook
EPUB Ebook

What is this book?

THE LAST FEW YEARS HAVE SEEN AN OVERWHELMING
AMOUNT OF FACTS, FIGURES, STATS AND CLAIMS THROWN
AT ALL OF US ABOUT THE SCOTTISH REFERENDUM. VOTERS
WE SPEAK TO ARE OFTEN CALLING FOR 'JUST THE FACTS';
NO POLITICAL BLUSTER OR CONFUSING JARGON. WITH THIS
BOOK, WE'VE TRIED TO FIND THESE FACTS, CUT THROUGH THE
SPIN AND CONFUSION, AND PRESENT THE CRUCIAL AREAS OF
DEBATE THAT AFFECT OUR LIVES AS CLEARLY AND SIMPLY AS
POSSIBLE.

     WHAT THIS BOOK IS <u>NOT</u>, IS A COMPREHENSIVE OR
IN-DEPTH GUIDE TO BOTH ARGUMENTS; IT'S OUR HOPE THAT
THESE FACTS SPUR YOU, THE READER, TO WANT TO FIND OUT
MORE, AND WE'VE INCLUDED SOME SOURCES AT THE BACK
OF THE BOOK. OUR INTENTION IS TO GIVE YOU A QUICK
INTRODUCTION TO THE KEY POINTS, AND AN OVERVIEW OF
THE MAIN ARGUMENTS IN CLEAR, SIMPLE-TO-UNDERSTAND
LANGUAGE. WE HAVE BEEN AS FAIR AS POSSIBLE TO BOTH
SIDES - HOWEVER, EDITING EXPANSIVE, OFTEN COMPLEX
ISSUES DOWN TO ONE PAGE MEANS WE HAVE TO SUMMARISE
DOCUMENTS OR STATEMENTS THAT IN THEIR ENTIRETY LAST
SEVERAL PAGES. WE HOPE YOU CAN APPRECIATE THAT —
AND IT'S WHY WE HOPE THESE PAGES ARE JUST THE START OF
A JOURNEY TOWARD HELPING YOU DECIDE THE WAY YOU'LL
VOTE IN THE REFERENDUM.

THE EDITORS, APRIL 2014.

What is the referendum?

ON SEPTEMBER 18TH 2014, ANYONE LIVING IN SCOTLAND WHO IS REGISTERED TO VOTE WILL BE ABLE TO VISIT A POLLING STATION AND BE ASKED THIS QUESTION:

SHOULD SCOTLAND BE AN INDEPENDENT COUNTRY?

YES   **NO**

ON EACH ISSUE, THE LEFT HAND PAGE OF THIS BOOK TELLS YOU THE IDEAS AND PLANS IF A MAJORITY OF PEOPLE ANSWER YES TO THAT QUESTION. THE RIGHT HAND PAGE TELLS YOU THE IDEAS AND PLANS IF THE ANSWER IS NO.

IF SCOTLAND VOTES YES, A SHORTHAND WAY OF DESCRIBING IT IS iScotland OR INDEPENDENT SCOTLAND, WHICH WE HAVE USED IN THIS BOOK; SIMILARLY, THE rUK WOULD BE THE REST OF THE UK, CONTINUING WITHOUT SCOTLAND.

WE REFER TO YES SCOTLAND AND THE SCOTTISH GOVERNMENT - ORGANISATIONS WHO SUPPORT INDEPENDENCE. WE ALSO REFER TO BETTER TOGETHER AND OTHER ORGANISATIONS WHO BELIEVE IN CONTINUING WITH THE UK UNION. WE ALSO REFER TO THE WHITE PAPER, A DOCUMENT THAT SETS OUT THE SCOTTISH GOVERNMENT'S VISION OF iScotland. MORE DETAILS ON THIS AND BETTER TOGETHER'S INFORMATION CAN BE FOUND AT THE BACK OF THE BOOK. WE HAVE, WHERE APPROPRIATE, NOTED WHO STATED THE FACT WE QUOTE, BUT ALL CITATIONS CAN BE FOUND ON THE WEBSITE LISTED AT THE BACK.

How To Vote

To vote in the Scottish independence referendum you must be aged 16 or over on 18th September 2014, and living in Scotland. You will also have to be either a British, qualifying Commonwealth or European Union citizen. A "qualifying Commonwealth citizen" is a person who is resident in the UK (in this case, Scotland) and has either leave to remain or enter the UK. Service personnel posted outside of Scotland, as well as their spouse or partner, and any 16 or 17 year old children, may also vote if they are registered to vote in Scotland. You must be registered to vote by 2nd September 2014.

You can vote in 3 different ways:

In person, at your local polling station, on 18th September.

By post, your vote arriving no later than 5pm, on the 3rd September 2014.

By proxy. If you cannot vote in person, you can nominate someone you trust to vote on your behalf. Your proxy nomination form must arrive no later than 5pm, on the 3rd September 2014.

Find out more at aboutmyvote.co.uk

ECONOMIC
ISSUES

ECONOMY

The White Paper states that tax receipts per person in Scotland are the same as the UK. After oil and gas tax, revenue per person in Scotland is roughly 20% higher than the UK.

In the last five years, Scotland's finances have been stronger than the UK as a whole by £12.6 billion.

The SNP has plans to negotiate a "currency union" with the UK - meaning Scotland can keep the £. In March 2014, a UK government minister secretly said that Scotland would be allowed to use the £.

The OECD places an iScotland as the 14th wealthiest nation in the world, by GDP per head.

ECONOMY

64% of all Scottish exports go to the rest of the UK. Scotland sells more to the rest of the UK than the rest of the world combined.

Institute for Fiscal Studies claims that budget cuts or tax rises of £3-10 billion would be needed to balance an iScotland's budget.

In January 2014, George Osborne stated the UK is not willing to enter a currency union with an independent Scotland; meaning Scotland could not use the £ as currency.

The CBI says that leaving the UK would "create risk, uncertainty for the Scottish economy, and would cost jobs."

OIL & GAS

The Scottish Government claims there is around £1 trillion of oil in the North Sea - around 15-24 million barrels.

The White Paper sets out a plan to create an 'oil-fund' - the Scottish Energy Fund - where tax money from oil is saved like Norway, which will reach $1 trillion in 2019.

The White Paper agrees with a report by Sir Ian Wood to create a new regulator of the oil and gas industries.

Over the next 30 years, 90% of all revenue producing fields will be in an iScotland.

OIL & GAS

Better Together claims that oil and gas would be 20% of an independent Scotland's income - compared to roughly 2% for the UK.

Volatile prices - the difference between the highest price for oil and lowest price for oil that the UK government has received is equivalent to the entire Scottish NHS budget.

The UK Government has agreed to adopt a new regulator for oil and gas - in line with Sir Ian Wood's report.

David Cameron stated that the "broad shoulders" of the UK were the only way to support future investment in the North Sea.

BUSINESS

Scottish government wants to offer a simpler, cheaper "utility" intellectual property protection scheme, being cheaper to access for SME's.

Boost high value job by increased manufacturing activity; The White Paper calls to reduce corporation tax by 3%.

Give SME's financial incentives through tax schemes, such as an increase in National Insurance employment allowance .

Establish a National Convention on Employment and Labour relations encouraging direct dialogue on topics like labour market reform and employment law. Abolish the Employee Ownership Schemes, which trades employee's rights on unfair dismissal/redundancy pay for shares.

YES

Supermarket bosses have said prices may rise for business and consumers on leaving UK.

If Scotland loses the UK Pound, jobs could be lost due to the cost of changing money to trade with the rUK.

36% of Scottish businesses say they "would consider" relocating if Scotland becomes independent.

In a survey, 44% of firms of all sizes said independence would harm their prospects.

ENERGY

The Scottish Government wants to tackle fuel poverty in Scotland more effectively by addressing the specific needs of Scottish consumers.

The White Paper calls for new models of community ownership of energy generation.

Scotland will continue to participate in the UK-wide market for electricity and gas.

Currently, consumers pay for Westminster policies to improve energy efficiency; the Scottish Government wants energy companies to foot this bill - claiming this will reduce bills by around five per cent, or around £70 every year.

ENERGY

As part of the UK, Better Together states we can pool and share our energy resources for the benefit of all.

Better Together states Scots benefit from a larger, stronger home energy market and therefore cheaper energy bills.

There is nothing that would require England and Wales to continue to buy energy from Scotland.

The security of energy supply for the future is better as part of a larger union with greater economic weight, says Better Together.

GLOBAL
ISSUES

THE EU

The Yes campaign believes that EU membership will be negotiated between the referendum and independence day, meaning Scotland never leaves the EU.

A French MP claimed Jose Manuel Barroso only intervened in the debate to try and secure a job as head of NATO. The Yes campaign say it is for countries in the EU to decide.

Nicola Sturgeon said that "Scotland is already in the EU and has been for 40 years" and therefore Scots have rights that mean they should stay part of the EU.

Alex Salmond has stated that Scotland would not use the Euro.

THE EU

The Better Together campaign believes that Scotland would have to negotiate to join the EU from the day of independence, if Scotland is allowed in at all.

President of the European Commision Jose Manuel Barroso said it would be "extremely difficult, if not impossible" for an independent Scotland to join.

Better Together state that the UK is one of the 'big three' countries in the EU; an independent Scotland wouldn't have the same influence as the current UK.

An independent Scotland would have to join the Euro, according to Better Together.

NO

IMMIGRATION

The Scottish Government wants to increase immigration.

Provide incentives to migrants who move to live and work in more remote geographical areas, while reintroducing the post-study work visa, meaning students who qualify here can stay to work.

With the Conservative Party's planned referendum on Europe, there could be possible exit from the EU and exclusion from the travel zone while some MP's want to pull out of the European convention on human rights.

The White Paper calls to end dawn raids on asylum seekers, and to close Dungavel detention centre.

IMMIGRATION

Better Together claim there could be an introduction of checkpoints and the need to show documents to cross the border with England if Scotland were to be independent.

The law is to be changed to mean a single power allows us to remove individuals who require, but do not have, leave to remain in the UK.

The UK government's overall aim is to decrease net migration, already down by 1/3 since its peak in 2010.

UK government opening up the Exceptional Talent visa route to world-leading individuals in the digital technology sector by enabling Tech City UK to endorse visa applications.

NO

DEFENCE

The Scottish Government wants to form the Scottish Defence Force - by "inheriting" the bases and buildings of the UK government - around £7.8 billion of assets.

Ban nuclear weapons from Scotland, convert Faslane, where the missiles are kept, into a conventional base. Wants to stay a member of NATO but only on the condition that nuclear weapons are not held in Scotland.

Wants to build up and maintain a defence force of around 15,000 personnel and 5,000 reservisists.

Bringing back the traditional regiment names lost in 2006.

YES

DEFENCE

The UK Government spends £34 billion on defence - more than 14 times the proposed defence budget of an independent Scotland.

Keep nuclear weapons on the Clyde. 15,000 people are currently directly or indirectly employed by Faslane.

Defence contractors BAE Systems said the Union offered "greater stability" and Babcock said independence created "risk and uncertainty."

Former GCHQ boss Sir David Omand warns that an independent Scotland cannot use the spy network of Britain and there was no guarantee that the UK would share intelligence.

NO

SOCIAL

ENVIRONMENT

The White Paper argues that Scotland will have the opportunity to enshrine protection of our environment in the proposed written constitution for Scotland.

Scottish Government will seek a better deal on Pillar 2 of the Common Agricultural Policy, allowing increased funding for environmental protection and emissions reduction.

Measures on energy production to be complemented by incentives for greater energy efficiency; minimising energy demand, reducing energy bills, through water efficiency and reducing waste.

Introduce a leasing system for offshore and onshore renewables.

YES

ENVIRONMENT

Investment in Scotland's green energy growth is paid for by 26 million households across the United Kingdom. In 2013, that subsidy was £37 per electricity bill per year, according to Consumer Focus Scotland.

The UK government are legally committed to meeting 15% of the UK's energy demand from renewable sources by 2020.

UK government is developing one of the most comprehensive programmes of carbon capture and storage in the world.

Committed to a programme of new nuclear power stations by 2019 to cut carbon emissions.

NO

HEALTH

The Scottish Government has promised protection of the frontline NHS budget.

The White Paper seeks greater scope and clearer powers to regulate alcohol and tobacco.

Yes Scotland says our national finances are healthier in relation to that of the rest of the United Kingdoms. This would mean we would be better able to afford the current level, and an increase, in NHS spending.

Create a distinct food standards policy linked to tax policy and advertising regulation.

HEALTH

Currently, any UK citizen has access to specialist treatment from anywhere in the United Kingdom - Better Together says there is uncertainty of this continuing in an iScotland.

Scotland already has control over healthcare issues through the Scottish Parliament.

The UK has recently agreed a UK/Chinese healthcare deal worth £120 million to the UK economy.

Consultation under way to introduce the Medical Innovation Bill, to increase the pace of responsible research across the NHS.

SOCIAL WELFARE

Extend the triple-lock on state pensions so they increase by either inflation, earnings or 2.5 per cent, whichever is higher.

Abolish the "bedroom tax", assisting 82,500 households in Scotland - including 63,500 households with a disabled adult and 15,500 households with children - to save an average of £50 per month.

Halt the further rollout of Universal Credit (UC) and Personal Independence Payment (PIP) in Scotland.

Ensure that benefits and tax credits increase in line with inflation to avoid the poorest families falling further into poverty.

YES

SOCIAL WELFARE

Continued rollout of Universal Credit across the UK.

By pooling our resources across the UK we can share the burden of funding and administering benefits across the broader shoulders of 60 million people across the UK rather than 5 million here in Scotland, says Better Together.

As part of the UK, benefit spending in Scotland is around 2% higher per head of population than for the rest of Great Britain.

Better Together says that the Scottish Government cannot guarantee a higher, or indeed the same, level of welfare spending in iScotland.

LAW

The White Paper calls on further work to improve control of airguns in Scotland. Firearms legislation could be simplified, making it easier for the public to understand and easier to enforce.

Powers to better tackle problem gambling through effective regulation of the industry.

Allow decisions on drugs policy and drug classification to be taken together.

Scotland's roads could be made safer through more appropriate penalties for drink driving, and powers for the police to conduct random breath tests any time, anywhere.

LAW

There are more powers already being devolved to the Scottish Parliament through the 2012 Scotland Act including a new Scottish rate of income tax.

The act also includes more power over regulating air weapons.

Scotland is already responsible for drink-driving and speed limits.

Better Together argues that as part of the UK we can have a strong Scottish Parliament with power over schools and hospitals, backed by the strength, security and stability that comes with being part of a bigger United Kingdom.

CULTURE/ARTS

Implement strategies to increase the numbers learning, speaking and using Gaelic.

A Scottish overseas diplomatic and trade network could provide Scotland with the opportunity to promote and share our culture and traditions with nations across the world.

All current licence fee payment exemptions and concessions, including those for people aged over 75 and for people who are sight-impaired, will be retained.

BBC's spend in Scotland in 2016/17 is estimated to be only around £175 million, half the budget planned under independence.

YES

CULTURE/ARTS

All Scottish cities currently have the chance to become UK City of Culture, boosting arts funding in the area.

We currently have our art recognised globally through the British Government Art Collection.

Culture is promoted through the internationally recognised British Council in over a hundred countries.

The UK government has announced Film Tax Relief will be available at 25% on the first £20 million of qualifying production expenditure and 20% thereafter, subsidising production for the UK film industry.

NO

COMMUNICATIONS

The White Paper also outlines a plan to turn the BBC in Scotland into the SBS, claiming it would have a larger budget than BBC Scotland currently.

The SNP intend to re-nationalise Royal Mail in Scotland after independence.

The White Paper calls for the Step Change programme to continue - with 95% of Scottish homes to have the option of broadband by 2017.

The White Paper outlines a plan to create a Scottish telecommunications body to oversee better 3G and 4G mobile services in Scotland, particularly in rural areas.

COMMUNICATIONS

Better Together state that there is no explanation from the Scottish Government of how they will renationalise or budget for Royal Mail in iScotland.

UK government is currently delivering a £530 million fund (with a further £250 million on which they recently consulted) to provide suitable broadband for rural communities.

A recently published Ofcom report states outdoor 3G coverage in Scotland is at 94% under UK government policies.

UK government will work with the 6 big companies that provide 90% of public wi-fi to introduce family friendly filters to public networks.

NO

RURAL AFFAIRS

The White Paper claims that Scotland's agriculture is a "low priority" for the UK at EU talks; Scotland receives 1.1% of the EU Fisheries Fund even though it catches 7% of Europe's fish each year.

Claims that an iScotland would have benefited from a law that by 2020 no EU country would receive less than 196 Euros per hectare of farming; could have brought Scotland an extra 1 billion over 6 years.

The Scottish Government argues smaller countries like Ireland are able to get much larger farm subsidies.

Bring forward an act to implement the findings of the Islands Areas Ministerial Working Groups.

YES